Dinner ☑

games ☐ The opening ☐

Bigo

other ☐

86100180R00062

Made in the USA
San Bernardino, CA
26 August 2018